NAVIGATING

NEURODIVERSITY

EMPOWERING TEENAGERS ON THE AUTISM SPECTRUM

BY

Judith Sterlin PhD

TABLE OF CONTENT

INTRODUCTION

Autism Spectrum Disorder (ASD) is a developmental condition that appears in various ways, presenting both challenges and strengths for those affected by it. The teenage years, with their significant changes and societal expectations, can be especially complex for teenagers on the autism spectrum. However, it is essential to acknowledge that neurodiversity is a natural and valuable aspect of human variation.

This comprehensive guide, titled "Navigating Neurodiversity: Empowering Teenagers on the Autism Spectrum," aims to provide insights, strategies, and support to teenagers, parents, educators, and professionals involved in the lives of autistic adolescents. By taking a strengths-based approach and promoting inclusivity, we can create an environment that fosters the overall development and well-being of teenagers with autism.

In this guide, we will explore the unique challenges faced by autistic teenagers, including social interactions, academics, and emotional regulation. We will emphasize the importance of creating a supportive environment that encourages understanding, acceptance, and inclusiveness. Additionally, we will discuss methods of empowering teenagers on the autism spectrum, focusing on self-advocacy, independence, and pursuing personal interests.

Parents and caregivers play a crucial role in the lives of autistic teenagers, and we will provide strategies and resources to help them understand and support their child's individual needs. Furthermore, we will address the important topic of mental health and well-being, offering guidance on managing anxiety, stress, and seeking professional help when necessary.

Transitioning into adulthood is a significant milestone, and we will explore various aspects such as post-secondary education, vocational opportunities, independent living, and legal rights. Moreover, this guide will share inspiring success stories and profiles of individuals who have thrived despite the challenges they faced.

Throughout this journey, we will highlight valuable resources, organizations, books, and support networks that can assist teenagers, parents, and professionals in their quest for empowerment and support. By promoting acceptance and celebrating neurodiversity, we can create a world where teenagers on the autism spectrum can thrive and contribute their unique talents and perspectives.

Let us embark on this empowering exploration together, embracing the strengths and potential of teenagers with autism, while creating a society that recognizes and supports their journey of self-discovery and personal growth.

CHAPTER 1

1.1 UNDERSTANDING AUTISM SPECTRUM DISORDER

Autism Spectrum Disorder (ASD) is a complex neurodevelopmental disorder that affects how a person thinks, communicates, and interacts with others. It is characterized by a wide range of symptoms and behaviors that can vary greatly from person to person. ASD is typically diagnosed in early childhood, although some individuals may not receive a diagnosis until later in life.

One of the key features of ASD is difficulties in social interaction and communication. People with ASD may have challenges in understanding and responding to social cues, maintaining eye contact, engaging in reciprocal conversations, and developing meaningful relationships. They may also exhibit repetitive behaviors, restricted interests, and sensory sensitivities. However, it is important to note that not all individuals with ASD will display the same symptoms or severity.

The causes of ASD are still not fully understood, but research suggests a combination of genetic and environmental factors may contribute to its development. There is no single known cause for ASD, and it is not caused by parenting or external environmental factors.

It is crucial to recognize that individuals with ASD have unique strengths and abilities as well. Many individuals with ASD possess exceptional attention to detail, excellent memory, and proficiency in specific areas of interest. Some may excel in mathematics, music, art, or computer programming, among other fields. It is essential to focus on nurturing these strengths and providing appropriate support and accommodations to help individuals with ASD reach their full potential.

Support and interventions for individuals with ASD can vary depending on their individual needs and challenges. Early intervention programs, such as speech therapy, occupational therapy, and behavioral interventions, can be highly beneficial in promoting communication, social skills, and independence. Additionally, a supportive and inclusive educational environment can make a significant difference in the lives of individuals with ASD.

It is important to foster understanding and acceptance of individuals with ASD within society. By promoting awareness, education, and inclusion, we can create a more inclusive and accommodating society that embraces the diversity of neurodivergent individuals.

1.2 EMBRACING THE DIVERSITY OF NEUROLOGICAL CONDITIONS

The concept of neurodiversity acknowledges and celebrates the natural range of human neurological development, encompassing conditions like autism, ADHD, dyslexia, and others. It emphasizes that neurological differences are a normal part of human diversity, rather than deficiencies or disorders requiring correction.

Regarding teenagers with autism, embracing neurodiversity involves recognizing and valuing their unique abilities and strengths. It shifts the focus from a deficit-oriented approach to one that appreciates the inherent talents and potentials of individuals with autism. By acknowledging and appreciating these strengths, society can provide opportunities for autistic teenagers to thrive and contribute in their own distinct ways.

Embracing neurodiversity also entails fostering inclusiveness and acceptance in various settings, such as schools, communities, and social environments. It means creating an environment where autistic teenagers feel understood, supported, and respected for who they are. Achieving this involves educating others, dispelling misconceptions about autism, and promoting empathy and tolerance.

By embracing neurodiversity, society can move away from attempting to "normalize" autistic individuals and instead focus on creating an environment that accommodates their unique needs and offers them equal opportunities to succeed. It encourages the development of inclusive educational practices that acknowledge and cater to diverse learning styles and strengths.

Furthermore, embracing neurodiversity is not just about accepting differences, but also about embracing the contributions and perspectives that autistic individuals bring to various aspects of life. Autistic teenagers often possess exceptional attention to detail, pattern recognition skills, creativity, and a unique problem-solving approach. These qualities can be harnessed and utilized in fields such as technology, art, science, and innovation, providing fresh insights and approaches.

In essence, embracing neurodiversity involves recognizing and appreciating the inherent value of neurological differences, including autism, and creating an inclusive and supportive environment that enables autistic teenagers to thrive. It is about celebrating their strengths, providing equal opportunities, and fostering a society that embraces and learns from the diverse perspectives and contributions of individuals on the autism spectrum.

Neurodiversity is a concept that challenges the prevailing notion that there is a standard or "normal" way for the human brain to function. Instead, it recognizes that neurological differences are a natural part of the human experience and should be embraced and celebrated. This shift in perspective has significant implications, particularly when it comes to teenagers on the autism spectrum.

When we embrace neurodiversity, we acknowledge that autism is not a disorder or a defect that needs to be fixed. Rather, it is a unique way of experiencing and interacting with the world. Autistic teenagers often have distinct abilities and strengths that can contribute positively to society. For example, they may possess remarkable attention to detail, a heightened sense of pattern recognition, and a different way of problem-solving that can lead to innovative solutions.

Unfortunately, many traditional approaches to education and support tend to focus on remediating deficits and trying to make autistic individuals conform to neurotypical norms. This can lead to feelings of exclusion, frustration, and a lack of opportunities for autistic teenagers to showcase their true potential. Embracing neurodiversity, on the other hand, involves recognizing and nurturing the unique strengths of autistic individuals, providing them with the necessary accommodations and support to thrive.

In educational settings, embracing neurodiversity means adopting inclusive practices that cater to diverse learning styles and strengths. It requires educators to understand and respect the individual needs of autistic students and create an environment that promotes their success. This could involve flexible learning approaches, sensory accommodations, and personalized support systems.

Beyond the classroom, embracing neurodiversity is about creating a society that values and appreciates the contributions of all individuals, regardless of their neurological differences. It requires a collective effort to break down barriers, challenge stereotypes, and promote inclusivity in all aspects of life. By fostering acceptance and understanding, we can create communities and social environments where autistic teenagers feel embraced, supported, and empowered to participate fully.

Embracing neurodiversity also calls for increased awareness and education about autism. It is crucial to dispel myths and misconceptions surrounding autism, promoting accurate information and understanding. This can help combat stigma and foster a more compassionate and empathetic society that values the diversity of human minds.

These are a paradigm shift that recognizes and celebrates the inherent value of neurological differences, including autism. It is about creating inclusive environments, providing equal opportunities, and nurturing the unique strengths and abilities of autistic teenagers. By doing so, we can build a society that not only accepts but also learns from and appreciates the diverse perspectives and contributions of

individuals on the autism spectrum.

CHAPTER 2

CHALLENGES FACED BY TEENAGERS WITH AUTISM

2.2 ACADEMIC AND EDUCATIONAL CHALLENGES:

Autistic teenagers may encounter specific challenges in academic settings that require targeted support and accommodations. These challenges can impact their learning, progress, and overall educational experience. Here are some key areas where they may face

difficulties:

2.2.1 EXECUTIVE FUNCTIONING SKILLS:

Many autistic teenagers struggle with executive functioning skills, which are essential for organizing, planning, and managing tasks. Difficulties in this area can manifest as challenges with time management, prioritizing tasks, initiating and completing assignments, and staying organized. These difficulties can impact their ability to meet deadlines, follow instructions, and effectively manage their academic workload.

To support autistic teenagers with executive functioning challenges, educators and parents can implement strategies such as breaking tasks into smaller, manageable steps, providing visual schedules and reminders, and using organizational tools such as checklists or digital planners. Teaching and reinforcing planning and time-management skills can also be beneficial in helping them navigate their academic responsibilities more

effectively.

2.2.2 TRANSITIONS AND CHANGES:

Transitions and changes in routine can be particularly challenging for autistic teenagers. They may struggle with adapting to new classroom environments, changes in teachers or classmates, and alterations in daily schedules. These transitions can lead to anxiety, stress, and difficulties in maintaining focus and engagement.

Creating a structured and predictable learning environment can help alleviate some of these challenges. Providing advance notice of upcoming changes or transitions, offering visual schedules or timetables, and gradually introducing new routines can support autistic teenagers in managing transitions more smoothly. Additionally, offering social stories or visual guides that explain what to expect during transitions can provide reassurance and enhance their understanding of the changes.

2.2.3 SENSORY SENSITIVITIES:

Many autistic teenagers experience sensory sensitivities, where certain sounds, sights, textures, or smells can be overwhelming or distracting. These sensitivities can affect their ability to concentrate, participate in classroom activities, and effectively process information. For example, a noisy classroom or bright fluorescent lights may cause sensory overload, making it difficult for them to focus on learning.

To address sensory sensitivities, educators can create a sensory-friendly classroom environment. This can involve providing options for sensory breaks, incorporating calming or fidget tools, using soft lighting, minimizing auditory distractions, and allowing flexible seating arrangements. Collaboration with occupational therapists or sensory integration specialists can also provide valuable insights and strategies for accommodating sensory needs in the classroom.

2.2.4 COMMUNICATION AND LANGUAGE:

Some autistic teenagers may face challenges with communication and language, which can impact their ability to understand and express themselves effectively. They may struggle with understanding complex instructions, reading comprehension, and written expression. Difficulties in verbal communication can also affect their ability to actively participate in classroom discussions and engage with peers.

Supporting communication and language skills in the academic setting can involve using visual supports, such as visual aids, graphic organizers, or written instructions, to enhance understanding. Providing additional time for processing and responding to questions can also be beneficial. Collaboration with speech-language pathologists or communication specialists can offer further strategies to support their language and communication needs.

Individualized support and accommodations are crucial in addressing the academic challenges faced by autistic teenagers. By implementing tailored strategies, educators and parents can create an inclusive learning environment that supports their academic progress, fosters their strengths, and helps them thrive in their educational journey.

To support autistic teenagers academically, it is essential to provide individualized support and accommodations. This can include:

- Developing an Individualized Education Program (IEP) or a 504 Plan that outlines specific accommodations and modifications to address their unique needs.
- Breaking down tasks into smaller, manageable steps and providing clear instructions.

- Offering visual supports, such as visual schedules, visual cues, and graphic organizers, to enhance understanding and organization.

- Creating a structured and predictable learning environment with consistent routines and clear expectations.

- Providing assistive technology tools, such as text-to-speech software or noise-cancelling headphones, to address sensory sensitivities.

Collaboration between teachers, parents, and professionals is crucial to identify and implement appropriate strategies and supports that promote the academic success of autistic teenagers. By addressing these challenges and providing tailored support, autistic teenagers can thrive academically and reach their full potential.

2.3 EMOTIONAL REGULATION AND MENTAL HEALTH: A REWRITTEN VERSION

Difficulties with emotional regulation and managing emotions effectively are common among many teenagers on the autism spectrum. These challenges have a significant impact on their overall well-being and daily functioning. The following key aspects are related to emotional regulation and mental health that autistic teenagers often encounter:

2.3.1 EMOTIONAL INTENSITY:

Autistic teenagers often experience intense emotions and are highly sensitive to both positive and negative experiences. They struggle with controlling their emotional responses, which can result in outbursts, meltdowns, or emotional shutdowns. These intense emotional reactions are often triggered by changes in routine, sensory overload, social interactions, or academic stress.

To support emotional regulation, it is crucial to equip autistic teenagers with tools and strategies to recognize and manage their emotions. This can involve teaching self-calming techniques like deep breathing exercises, taking sensory breaks, or utilizing visual aids to identify and express their emotions. Creating a safe and supportive environment where they feel comfortable expressing their emotions is also essential for their emotional well-being.

2.3.2 ANXIETY AND STRESS:

Autistic teenagers are more susceptible to anxiety and stress due to challenges in social interactions, sensory sensitivities, and academic demands. They struggle to cope with uncertainty, unexpected changes, or overwhelming situations. Anxiety often presents itself as increased rigidity, avoidance behaviors, or physical symptoms such as stomachaches or headaches.

Supporting autistic teenagers in managing anxiety and stress requires developing personalized coping strategies. This may involve teaching relaxation techniques, establishing predictable routines, providing opportunities for breaks or sensory regulation, and helping them build problem-solving skills. Encouraging open communication and creating a safe space for expressing worries or concerns can also help reduce anxiety levels.

2.3.3 MENTAL HEALTH CONCERNS:

Autistic teenagers face a higher risk of experiencing mental health conditions such as depression, anxiety disorders, or attention-deficit/hyperactivity disorder (ADHD). The challenges they encounter in social interactions, academic settings, and sensory experiences contribute to feelings of loneliness, low self-esteem, and difficulties with self-identity. It is crucial to prioritize mental health support and intervene early for these individuals.

Collaborating with mental health professionals experienced in working with autistic individuals, such as psychologists or therapists, is instrumental in addressing mental health concerns. Providing access to counseling services, therapeutic interventions, and support groups can equip them with valuable tools for managing and improving their mental well-being.

It is vital for parents, educators, and professionals to remain vigilant about changes in behavior or mood that may indicate underlying mental health concerns. Building a supportive network that includes family, friends, and trusted adults can establish a strong support system for autistic teenagers, ensuring that their emotional well-being is a top priority.

By addressing the emotional regulation and mental health needs of autistic teenagers, we empower them to develop effective coping strategies, enhance their overall well-being, and navigate challenges with resilience and self-compassion.

CHAPTER 3

3.1 BUILDING A SUPPORTIVE ENVIRONMENT

Creating a supportive environment entails establishing inclusive schools and communities that cater to the needs of teenagers with autism. Inclusive settings promote a sense of acceptance, understanding, and belonging, enabling autistic teenagers to flourish and realize their full potential. The following are essential strategies for fostering inclusivity in schools and communities:

3.1.1 RAISING AWARENESS AND EDUCATION:

It is crucial to increase awareness and provide education about autism spectrum disorder to create an inclusive environment. Educators, students, parents, and community members should have access to accurate and up-to-date information about autism, including its characteristics, strengths, and challenges. This knowledge helps dispel misconceptions, reduce stigma, and encourage empathy and understanding.

Educators can enhance their understanding of effective teaching strategies, accommodations, and support techniques for autistic students through professional development opportunities. Establishing a culture of continuous learning and promoting collaboration among school staff further strengthens inclusive practices.

3.1.2 PROMOTING PEER SUPPORT AND ACCEPTANCE:

Promoting peer support and acceptance is vital for fostering an inclusive school environment. Encouraging friendships, empathy, and understanding among students creates a sense of belonging for autistic teenagers. Implementing peer mentorship programs or buddy systems provides opportunities for neurotypical students to support their autistic peers and vice versa, fostering a culture of inclusion and collaboration.

School-wide initiatives, such as autism awareness campaigns, assemblies, or special events, help promote acceptance and understanding among the entire student body. Celebrating neurodiversity and highlighting the unique strengths and talents of autistic individuals contribute to a more inclusive and accepting school community.

3.1.3 BUILDING COLLABORATIVE PARTNERSHIPS:

Collaborative partnerships among schools, families, and the wider community are crucial for creating a supportive environment for autistic teenagers. Establishing open lines of communication and fostering positive relationships among parents, educators, and community organizations ensure a coordinated and comprehensive approach to supporting autistic students.

Engaging with autism support organizations, advocacy groups, and local service providers offers valuable resources, expertise, and opportunities for collaboration. These partnerships facilitate access to specialized services, promote community inclusion, and provide ongoing support to autistic teenagers and their families.

3.1.4 CREATING AN ACCESSIBLE PHYSICAL AND SENSORY ENVIRONMENT:

Designing a physical environment that considers the sensory needs of autistic teenagers significantly impacts their well-being and comfort. Providing quiet spaces, sensory-friendly classrooms, and designated areas for breaks or sensory regulation helps minimize sensory overload and promotes a conducive learning environment.

Modifying the physical environment to reduce sensory distractions, such as utilizing natural lighting, minimizing visual clutter, or incorporating calming elements, enhances the overall comfort and focus of autistic students. Additionally, ensuring accessibility and inclusive design principles, such as ramps, visual aids, or assistive technology, further promotes inclusivity for all students.

By actively working towards creating inclusive schools and communities, we can offer the necessary support, acceptance, and opportunities for autistic teenagers to thrive. Cultivating a culture of inclusivity, understanding, and collaboration benefits not only individuals with autism but also fosters a sense of belonging and diversity for the entire school and community.

3.2 ENHANCING COMMUNICATION AND SOCIAL SKILLS:

Improving communication and social skills is crucial for autistic teenagers as it enables them to effectively interact in social situations, form relationships, and fully participate in various social contexts. By enhancing these skills, we can greatly contribute to their overall well-being and success. Below are some strategies to foster the development of these skills:

3.2.1 SOCIAL SKILLS TRAINING:

Structured programs that focus on social skills training can provide autistic teenagers with supportive environments to learn and practice important social skills. These programs typically concentrate on skills like initiating and maintaining conversations, understanding nonverbal cues, perspective-taking, and resolving conflicts.

Social skills training can be conducted through organized group sessions led by trained professionals, where teenagers engage in role-playing, social scenarios, and guided discussions. Additionally, personalized coaching or mentoring can be beneficial, providing individualized support and feedback tailored to each teenager's specific needs.

3.2.2 VISUAL SUPPORTS:

Visual aids play a critical role in enhancing communication and social interactions for autistic teenagers. Utilizing visual supports, such as social stories, visual schedules, or cue cards, provides concrete and visual information that aids understanding and facilitates communication.

Visual supports help autistic teenagers navigate social expectations, comprehend abstract concepts, and anticipate social routines or changes.

They can also be used to teach social rules, clarify expectations, and facilitate communication across various settings, including the classroom, community, or home.

3.2.3 PEER MODELING AND INCLUSION:

Involving neurotypical peers in social activities and interactions offers valuable opportunities for autistic teenagers to observe and learn from their peers' social skills. Peer modeling enables autistic teenagers to observe and imitate appropriate social behaviors, communication styles, and social cues.

Encouraging inclusive social opportunities, such as group projects, clubs, or extracurricular activities, can facilitate positive social interactions and friendships. Promoting an inclusive culture that values diversity, acceptance, and empathy among all students helps create an environment where autistic teenagers feel comfortable and supported.

3.2.4 INDIVIDUALIZED COMMUNICATION SUPPORTS:

Recognizing and accommodating the unique communication needs of autistic teenagers is crucial for their social development. Some individuals may benefit from alternative communication methods, such as visual supports, augmentative and alternative communication (AAC) devices, or social scripts.

Individualized communication supports should be tailored to each teenager's specific strengths, preferences, and needs. Collaborating with speech-language pathologists or communication specialists can provide valuable guidance and strategies for supporting their communication development.

3.2.5 SOCIAL SKILLS IN NATURAL SETTINGS:

While structured social skills training is beneficial, it is equally important to provide opportunities for autistic teenagers to practice their skills in natural settings. Real-life experiences allow them to apply their skills, adapt to different social contexts, and gain confidence in their abilities.

Creating inclusive environments that encourage social interactions, offer collaboration opportunities, and promote positive peer relationships can foster the development of communication and social skills. Teachers, parents, and community members can support these experiences by facilitating inclusive group activities, promoting cooperative learning, and encouraging positive social interactions both within and outside the school environment.

By focusing on enhancing communication and social skills, we can empower autistic teenagers to establish meaningful connections, navigate social interactions, and actively engage in their communities. Through targeted interventions, personalized support, and the creation of inclusive environments, we can help them develop the skills and confidence necessary for social success.

CHAPTER 4

EMPOWERING AUTISTIC TEENAGERS: SPEAKING UP AND MAKING CHOICES

4.1 SELF-ADVOCACY AND SELF-DETERMINATION:

Empowering teenagers on the autism spectrum involves helping them develop skills in speaking up for themselves and making choices that shape their lives. Speaking up for oneself means expressing needs, preferences, and rights, while making choices refers to the ability to decide and shape one's own path. By supporting autistic teenagers in developing these skills, we can help them become active participants in their lives and advocates for their needs. Here are important aspects related to speaking up for oneself and making choices:

4.1.1 UNDERSTANDING AND EMBRACING AUTISM:

The journey of speaking up for oneself starts with understanding and accepting one's autism. It is crucial to provide autistic teenagers with age-appropriate information about autism, including its strengths, challenges, and the diverse experiences within the autism community. By promoting a positive self-image and encouraging self-acceptance, they can develop a strong sense of identity rooted in their unique neurological characteristics.

Encourage open discussions about autism, recognizing and appreciating their distinct perspectives, talents, and strengths. Help them understand that their experiences are valid and valuable, fostering pride in their identity as autistic individuals.

4.1.2 DEVELOPING EFFECTIVE

Communication Skills:

Effective communication is essential for self-advocacy. Autistic teenagers should be supported in developing communication skills that allow them to express their thoughts, feelings, and needs clearly and confidently. This includes both verbal and nonverbal communication, active listening, and understanding social cues.

Encourage the use of visual supports, such as visual schedules, social stories, or communication aids, to enhance communication and understanding. Role-playing and practicing real-life situations can help them develop effective communication strategies for different scenarios.

4.1.3 RECOGNIZING STRENGTHS AND INTERESTS:

Self-advocacy becomes stronger when individuals recognize their strengths, interests, and goals. Assist autistic teenagers in identifying their unique talents and passions by providing opportunities for exploration and self-discovery. Encourage them to set personal goals, both short-term and long-term, and support their pursuit of their aspirations.

Engage in conversations about their interests and help them understand how their strengths and passions can be channeled into meaningful endeavors. This process of self-discovery and goal-setting nurtures a sense of purpose and self-advocacy as they work towards achieving their dreams.

4.1.4 BUILDING SELF-CONFIDENCE AND RESILIENCE:

Developing self-confidence and resilience is crucial for self-advocacy. Encourage autistic teenagers to recognize their achievements, celebrate their strengths, and embrace their uniqueness. Provide positive reinforcement and create a supportive environment that encourages them to take risks and learn from setbacks.

Assist them in developing problem-solving skills and coping strategies to navigate challenges and setbacks. Promote a growth mindset that emphasizes the importance of learning from mistakes and embracing personal growth.

4.1.5 COLLABORATING WITH SUPPORT NETWORKS:

Collaborating with support networks is vital for effective self-advocacy. Encourage autistic teenagers to identify trusted adults, such as parents, teachers, mentors, or support groups, who can offer guidance, support, and resources. Help them understand that seeking assistance is a strength, not a weakness.

Support networks can help navigate challenges, access services and accommodations, and understand legal rights and entitlements. Encourage regular communication and collaboration with these networks to ensure ongoing support and guidance in their self-advocacy journey.

By fostering skills in self-advocacy and making choices, we empower autistic teenagers to have a voice, make informed decisions, and advocate for their needs and rights. These skills serve as a foundation for their journey towards greater independence, self-confidence, and a fulfilling future.

4.2 STRENGTHENING INDEPENDENCE AND LIFE SKILLS:

Enhancing the independence and life skills of teenagers on the autism spectrum is crucial for empowering them to tackle the daily obstacles they face and prepare for adulthood. By equipping them with vital skills, we can nurture their self-reliance, confidence, and ability to lead fulfilling lives independently. Here are the key aspects related to strengthening independence and life skills:

4.2.1 DEVELOPING DAILY LIVING SKILLS:

Daily living skills encompass a range of tasks necessary for personal care, managing households, and maintaining overall well-being. It is important to support autistic teenagers in developing and practicing these skills to enhance their independence. Essential daily living skills include personal hygiene, meal preparation, grocery shopping, household chores, managing finances, and transportation.

Breaking down these skills into smaller, manageable steps and using visual aids like checklists or schedules can facilitate learning and reinforce independence. Providing opportunities for hands-on practice in real-life situations and gradually increasing responsibilities as their confidence grows can be beneficial.

4.2.2 MANAGING TIME AND BEING ORGANIZED:

Time management and organizational skills are crucial for effectively handling responsibilities, schedules, and tasks. Autistic teenagers can benefit from learning strategies to plan and prioritize activities, set goals, meet deadlines, and stay organized. Useful techniques include using calendars or planners, creating to-do lists, breaking tasks into smaller steps, and utilizing visual aids.

Teaching them how to estimate time, allocate resources, and balance competing priorities promotes their independence and productivity. Implementing clear routines and consistent structures can also help manage time and reduce anxiety.

4.2.3 PROBLEM-SOLVING AND DECISION-MAKING:

Developing problem-solving and decision-making skills empowers autistic teenagers to overcome challenges and make informed choices. By teaching them problem-solving techniques such as breaking problems down, brainstorming solutions, and evaluating alternatives, we help build their resilience and critical thinking abilities.

Encouraging them to consider different options, weigh pros and cons, and anticipate potential outcomes when making decisions is important. It is crucial to create a supportive environment that allows for mistakes and learning from them, as this promotes growth and confidence in problem-solving.

4.2.4 SOCIAL AND INTERPERSONAL SKILLS:

Social and interpersonal skills are essential for establishing relationships, collaborating with others, and navigating social situations. Autistic teenagers can benefit from learning and practicing skills such as active listening, empathy, conflict resolution, and assertiveness. Role-playing and social skills training programs can provide valuable opportunities to improve their social interaction abilities.

Encouraging them to participate in social activities, join clubs or organizations related to their interests, and develop connections with peers who share similar hobbies or goals is beneficial. Building a supportive social network fosters their sense of belonging and provides a platform for practicing and refining social skills.

4.2.5 TECHNOLOGY AND ASSISTIVE TOOLS:

Utilizing technology and assistive tools can significantly support autistic teenagers in strengthening their independence. Various apps, software, and devices can assist with organization, time management, communication, and daily living tasks. Introducing them to assistive technology options that cater to their specific needs and preferences enhances their autonomy and efficiency.

Seeking guidance and recommendations from occupational therapists or technology specialists can provide additional support in identifying appropriate assistive tools for specific areas of need.

By focusing on strengthening independence and life skills, we enable autistic teenagers to take control of their lives, make informed choices, and confidently navigate daily challenges. These skills form a solid foundation for their future success and fulfillment.

4.3 EXPLORING INTERESTS AND TALENTS: A REWRITTEN VERSION

The exploration of interests and talents holds significant importance in empowering teenagers with autism. It enables them to uncover their passions, nurture their strengths, and find avenues for self-expression and personal satisfaction. By providing support and encouragement during this exploration, we can assist them in developing a strong sense of identity, boosting self-confidence, and cultivating a positive outlook on their abilities. Here are key aspects related to the exploration of interests and talents:

4.3.1 ENCOURAGING SELF-EXPRESSION:

Facilitating self-expression plays a pivotal role in the growth of autistic teenagers. Encourage them to engage in various creative forms of expression, such as art, music, writing, or drama. These creative activities provide a means for them to communicate their thoughts, emotions, and ideas in unique ways.

Create an environment that values and supports their creative pursuits, offering opportunities for them to showcase their work. Encourage them to experiment with different mediums and techniques, while celebrating their individuality and creativity.

4.3.2 IDENTIFYING INTERESTS AND STRENGTHS:

Assist autistic teenagers in discovering their interests and strengths by exposing them to a wide range of activities and experiences. Encourage them to try different hobbies, join clubs or groups related to their interests, and explore new areas of knowledge. Pay attention to their preferences and observe activities that captivate their attention and bring them joy.

Engage in conversations about their interests, asking open-ended questions to delve deeper into their passions. By actively listening and supporting their exploration, you can help them gain a clearer understanding of their interests and strengths.

4.3.3 CULTIVATING SKILLS AND EXPERTISE:

Once interests are identified, provide opportunities for autistic teenagers to cultivate their skills and expertise in those areas. Encourage them to set goals and create a plan for skill development. This may involve enrolling in classes, seeking mentorship, or accessing resources and learning materials.

Acknowledge and celebrate their progress along the way. Recognize their

efforts and offer constructive feedback
to help them refine their skills and reach
their full potential.

4.3.4 PROMOTING INCLUSION AND COMMUNITY ENGAGEMENT:

Promote inclusion and community engagement by connecting autistic teenagers with like-minded individuals who share their interests. Encourage their participation in clubs, organizations, or online communities where they can interact with peers who have similar hobbies or talents.

Inclusive environments provide opportunities for social interaction, collaboration, and the sharing of experiences and knowledge. Being part of a supportive community fosters a sense of belonging and can enhance their self-esteem.

4.3.5 BUILDING PATHWAYS TO FUTURE OPPORTUNITIES:

Exploring interests and talents can open doors to future opportunities and potential career paths. Help autistic teenagers connect their passions to real-world possibilities. Conduct research and engage in discussions about different professions, industries, and educational pathways that align with their interests.

Encourage them to seek internships, mentorships, or volunteering experiences in their areas of interest. These opportunities provide valuable exposure, networking possibilities, and practical experiences that can shape their future goals.

By actively supporting the exploration of interests and talents, we empower autistic teenagers to discover their passions, develop their skills, and establish a sense of purpose. This process helps them recognize their unique abilities and provides a solid

foundation for personal growth,

fulfillment, and future success.

CHAPTER 5

STRATEGIES FOR PARENTS AND CAREGIVERS

5.1: UNDERSTANDING AND SUPPORTING TEENAGERS WITH AUTISM

Parents and caregivers have a vital role in the lives of teenagers with autism. It is crucial to have a comprehensive understanding of their unique needs, strengths, and challenges in order to provide effective support and promote their overall well-being. This section offers strategies for parents and caregivers to enhance their comprehension and assistance for

teenagers with autism:

5.1.1: EDUCATE YOURSELF ABOUT AUTISM

Proactively educate yourself about autism spectrum disorder. Familiarize yourself with the common characteristics and traits associated with autism, as well as the diverse range of experiences within the autism community. This knowledge will enable you to gain a deeper understanding of your teenager's perspective and inform your approach to supporting them.

Engage in activities such as reading books, attending workshops, joining support groups, and accessing reliable online resources that provide information on autism. Additionally, seek opportunities to interact with professionals and connect with other parents to gain valuable insights and perspectives.

5.1.2: FOSTER OPEN AND POSITIVE COMMUNICATION

Maintain open and positive lines of communication with your teenager. Create a safe and non-judgmental environment where they feel comfortable expressing their thoughts, emotions, and concerns. Practice active listening and validate their experiences.

Encourage open dialogue about autism, allowing them to ask questions and share their own understanding of their condition. By fostering open communication, you can build trust, strengthen your relationship, and better support their needs.

5.1.3: TAILOR SUPPORT TO THEIR NEEDS

Recognize that each teenager with autism is unique, with their own individual strengths, challenges, and preferences. Customize your support to address their specific needs, taking into account their particular interests, sensory sensitivities, communication styles, and learning preferences.

Observe and learn which strategies work best for them in various situations. Adjust your approach accordingly, offering personalized support and accommodations that foster their independence and well-being.

5.1.4: ESTABLISH PREDICTABLE ROUTINES

Establishing structured and predictable routines can be beneficial for teenagers with autism. Create consistent daily routines and clearly communicate expectations to provide them with a sense of security and stability. Utilize visual aids such as schedules or visual timers to help them understand and anticipate daily activities and transitions.

Introduce changes or new experiences gradually, providing ample preparation and support. By preparing them for upcoming events or changes, you can help alleviate anxiety and facilitate smoother transitions.

5.1.5: PROMOTE SOCIAL OPPORTUNITIES

Encourage social opportunities for your teenager, allowing them to develop and practice their social skills. Support their participation in activities, clubs, or programs that align with their interests, providing opportunities for social interaction with peers who share similar hobbies or goals.

Collaborate with educators and community organizations to create inclusive environments that foster acceptance and understanding. Facilitate social skills training or groups that offer guidance and practice in navigating social situations.

5.1.6: PRIORITIZE SELF-CARE

Supporting a teenager with autism can be demanding, so it is essential to prioritize your own well-being. Allocate time for self-care and seek support from friends, family, or support groups who understand your experiences.

Take advantage of available resources and services that offer respite care or assistance. By taking care of your physical and mental health, you will be better equipped to support your teenager.

Remember, each teenager with autism is unique, and what works for one may not work for another. Maintain patience, adaptability, and a willingness to learn from your teenager. Seek professional guidance when necessary and collaborate with a multidisciplinary team to ensure comprehensive support.

By understanding and supporting your teenager with autism, you can provide them with the foundation they need to thrive, grow, and reach their full potential. Your dedication and advocacy will have a significant impact on their lives.

5.2 COLLABORATION WITH EDUCATORS AND PROFESSIONALS:

Effective collaboration with educators and professionals is crucial for ensuring that teenagers with autism receive the necessary support in educational settings. By working together as a team, parents and caregivers can help create a supportive and inclusive environment that promotes their teenager's academic and social development. Here are strategies for successful collaboration with educators and professionals:

5.2.1 ESTABLISHING OPEN AND TRANSPARENT COMMUNICATION:

Building open lines of communication with your teenager's educators and professionals is essential. Share information about your teenager's strengths, challenges, and specific support needs. Take the initiative to provide updates and insights that contribute to their understanding of your teenager's unique characteristics.

Create regular opportunities for meetings or check-ins to discuss progress, concerns, and strategies. Emphasize the importance of open dialogue, collaboration, and a shared commitment to your teenager's well-being and success.

5.2.2 SHARING INSIGHTS AND STRATEGIES:

As a parent or caregiver, you have valuable insights into your teenager's strengths, interests, and effective strategies for support. Share this information with educators and professionals to enhance their understanding of your teenager and their learning style.

Collaboratively develop and implement consistent strategies that can be used both at home and in school. This may involve using visual aids, sensory accommodations, or communication tools to support your teenager's engagement and participation.

5.2.3 ACTIVE PARTICIPATION IN INDIVIDUALIZED EDUCATION PROGRAM (IEP) MEETINGS:

Take an active role in the development and review of your teenager's Individualized Education Program (IEP). These meetings provide an opportunity to discuss goals, accommodations, and modifications that support your teenager's learning and development.

Come prepared with insights, suggestions, and questions. Collaborate with educators and professionals to establish meaningful goals, determine appropriate support measures, and monitor progress. Ensure that the IEP reflects your teenager's strengths, interests, and aspirations.

5.2.4 ADVOCATING FOR INCLUSIVE PRACTICES:

Advocate for inclusive practices within the educational setting. Encourage educators and professionals to create a welcoming and inclusive environment where all students, including those with autism, feel accepted and valued.

Promote awareness and understanding of autism among school staff and students. Share resources, organize workshops, or invite guest speakers to facilitate professional development opportunities that enhance knowledge and sensitivity towards autism.

5.2.5 SEEKING PROFESSIONAL EXPERTISE:

Recognize the expertise of educators and professionals in supporting students with autism. Consult specialists such as speech and language therapists, occupational therapists, or behavioral analysts, who can provide valuable insights and recommendations.

Collaborate with these professionals to align strategies and interventions between home and school. Seek their guidance in addressing specific challenges or developing individualized support measures that facilitate your teenager's learning and development.

5.2.6 FOSTERING A POSITIVE RELATIONSHIP:

Cultivate a positive and collaborative relationship with your teenager's educators and professionals. Acknowledge and appreciate their dedication and expertise in supporting your teenager's educational journey.

Maintain a respectful and constructive approach when discussing concerns or exploring alternative strategies. By fostering a positive relationship based on trust and mutual respect, you can effectively work together to support your teenager's growth and success.

Remember that collaboration with educators and professionals is an ongoing process. Regular communication, active involvement, and a shared commitment to your teenager's well-being and progress are key to creating a supportive and inclusive educational environment.

By working as a team, including parents, caregivers, educators, and professionals, we can ensure that teenagers with autism receive the necessary support to thrive academically, socially, and emotionally. Together, we can create a positive and enriching educational experience that sets the stage for their future success.

5.3 PROMOTING A POSITIVE RELATIONSHIP BETWEEN PARENTS AND TEENAGERS:

It is crucial to maintain a positive relationship between parents and teenagers with autism in order to promote their well-being and overall development. Creating a strong bond based on trust, communication, and understanding can establish a supportive environment where teenagers feel secure, valued, and empowered. Here are some strategies for fostering a positive parent-teenager relationship:

5.3.1 FACILITATING EFFECTIVE COMMUNICATION:

Establish open and effective channels of communication with your teenager. Encourage them to express their thoughts, feelings, and opinions, and actively listen to what they have to say. Create a safe and non-judgmental space where they feel comfortable sharing their experiences.

Adapt your communication style to meet their needs, considering their individual communication preferences and using clear and concise language. Utilize visual aids, social stories, or assistive communication devices as necessary.

5.3.2 VALIDATING AND SHOWING EMPATHY:

Validate your teenager's emotions and experiences, recognizing the challenges they may encounter. Show empathy and understanding, conveying that their perspective is valued. Acknowledge and validate their strengths, achievements, and efforts, which boosts their self-esteem and confidence.

Avoid minimizing or dismissing their feelings. Instead, offer support and reassurance during difficult times. By validating their experiences, you build trust and establish a foundation for open and honest communication.

5.3.3 SETTING CLEAR BOUNDARIES:

Establish clear and reasonable boundaries for your teenager, providing structure and guidance. Clearly communicate your expectations and rules, while also granting them a sense of autonomy and independence. Collaboratively establish boundaries that promote their safety, well-being, and personal growth.

Regularly revisit and discuss these boundaries, making adjustments as necessary. Engage in open conversations about the reasons behind specific rules, fostering understanding and cooperation.

5.3.4 ENCOURAGING AUTONOMY AND DECISION-MAKING:

Promote autonomy and self-determination in your teenager. Encourage them to make decisions and involve them in choices that affect their lives. Provide opportunities for them to practice decision-making skills, gradually increasing their independence and responsibility.

Support their interests and passions, allowing them to explore their own identity and pursue activities that align with their strengths and aspirations. Foster a sense of ownership over their life choices and celebrate their achievements, regardless of the outcome.

5.3.5 ENGAGING IN QUALITY TIME AND BONDING ACTIVITIES:

Dedicate time to shared activities and quality bonding experiences with your teenager. Participate in activities that they enjoy, such as hobbies, games, or outings. These moments create opportunities for connection, laughter, and the formation of lasting memories.

Be flexible and accommodate your teenager's preferences and sensory needs. Respect their need for downtime or solitude when necessary, while also finding a balance that ensures regular moments of connection.

5.3.6 PRACTICING SELF-CARE:

Prioritize self-care as a parent or caregiver to maintain a positive parent-teenager relationship. Engage in activities that rejuvenate and recharge you. Seek support from friends, family, or support groups who understand your experiences.

By practicing self-care, you can approach your interactions with your teenager with patience, understanding, and emotional resilience. Your own well-being directly impacts the dynamics of your relationship.

Remember that building a positive parent-teenager relationship is an ongoing process that requires patience, understanding, and adaptability. Each teenager is unique, and the dynamics of your relationship will evolve over time. By prioritizing open communication, empathy, and shared experiences, you can foster a relationship that supports your teenager's growth, self-confidence, and overall well-being.

CHAPTER 6

MENTAL HEALTH AND WELL-BEING

6.1: IDENTIFICATION AND MANAGEMENT OF ANXIETY AND DEPRESSION:

The mental well-being of teenagers with autism is vital to their overall health. It is important for parents, caregivers, and professionals to remain vigilant in recognizing and addressing mental health challenges such as anxiety and depression. Here are strategies for identifying and managing anxiety and depression in teenagers on the autism spectrum:

6.1.1 UNDERSTANDING ANXIETY AND DEPRESSION:

Gain knowledge about the signs, symptoms, and underlying causes of anxiety and depression in individuals with autism. Understand that anxiety and depression can manifest differently in autistic teenagers compared to their neurotypical peers.

Anxiety may appear as excessive worry, restlessness, irritability, disrupted sleep, or avoidance of specific situations.

Depression may be characterized by persistent sadness, loss of interest in activities, changes in appetite or sleep patterns, low energy, or thoughts of self-harm.

6.1.2 CREATING A SUPPORTIVE AND SAFE ENVIRONMENT:

Establish a supportive and safe environment where your teenager feels comfortable expressing their emotions and concerns without fear of judgment. Foster open communication and actively listen to their feelings and experiences.

Implement predictable routines, clear expectations, and a calm atmosphere to minimize anxiety triggers. Consider

sensory sensitivities and provide

sensory supports to help regulate

emotions and promote relaxation.

6.1.3 TEACHING COPING STRATEGIES:

Educate your teenager about coping strategies to manage anxiety and depression. Equip them with a range of techniques they can utilize when feeling overwhelmed. These may include deep breathing exercises, mindfulness techniques, sensory self-regulation activities, or engaging in hobbies that promote relaxation.

Encourage the use of visual supports, such as social stories or visual schedules, to aid their understanding and navigation of challenging situations. Teach problem-solving skills to empower them to tackle difficulties and find solutions.

6.1.4 SEEKING PROFESSIONAL SUPPORT:

If your teenager's anxiety or depression significantly affects their daily functioning or quality of life, consider seeking professional support. Consult with mental health professionals experienced in working with individuals on the autism spectrum.

Psychologists, psychiatrists, or therapists can provide specialized interventions like cognitive-behavioral therapy (CBT), social skills training, or medication management if necessary. Collaborate with these professionals to develop a customized treatment plan that addresses your teenager's specific needs.

6.1.5 ENCOURAGING SOCIAL CONNECTIONS:

Support your teenager in establishing and maintaining social connections. Peer support can contribute to a sense of belonging and reduce feelings of isolation. Encourage their participation in social activities, clubs, or support groups specifically designed for individuals with autism.

Work together with educators and professionals to create inclusive social opportunities within the school or community. Foster friendships and facilitate social skills training to enhance social interactions and reduce social anxiety.

6.1.6 PROMOTING A HEALTHY LIFESTYLE:

Promote a healthy lifestyle that includes regular physical activity, nutritious meals, and sufficient sleep. Engaging in physical exercise can help alleviate anxiety and improve mood. Encourage your teenager to participate in activities they enjoy, such as sports, yoga, or dance.

Ensure they maintain a balanced diet that supports their overall well-being.

Establish a consistent sleep routine that allows for adequate rest, as lack of sleep can worsen symptoms of anxiety and depression.

6.1.7 PROVIDING EMOTIONAL SUPPORT:

Offer continuous emotional support to your teenager. Validate their feelings and let them know you are there to listen and assist. Encourage them to express their emotions in healthy ways, such as through journaling, art, or confiding in a trusted adult.

Set an example by demonstrating positive coping skills and self-care practices in your own life, emphasizing the importance of taking care of mental health. Encourage them to seek support when needed, whether from family, friends, or professionals.

Remember that addressing anxiety and depression in autistic teenagers requires a comprehensive approach that incorporates a variety of strategies. It is crucial to customize these strategies to meet your teenager's individual needs. Regularly assess their well-being and make necessary adjustments.

Additionally, fostering a positive and supportive environment at home and in the community is crucial for their overall mental health. Encourage understanding, acceptance, and inclusivity among family members, peers, and educators. Celebrate their strengths and accomplishments to nurture their self-worth and resilience.

Keep in mind that progress may be gradual, and setbacks are a normal part of the journey. Be patient and persistent in supporting your teenager's mental health. Seek guidance and support from mental health professionals, autism organizations, and support networks that can provide valuable resources and assistance.

By actively recognizing and managing anxiety and depression in autistic teenagers, you can help them develop effective coping mechanisms, enhance their quality of life, and promote overall well-being. With your support and a collaborative approach, they can navigate their mental health challenges and thrive in all aspects of their lives.

6.2 STRESS MANAGEMENT TECHNIQUES PARAPHRASED:

Adolescents on the autism spectrum often experience stress as they face the trials of adolescence while managing the particularities of autism. It is crucial for them to learn effective stress management techniques that empower them to cope with daily stressors and enhance their overall well-being. Here are some strategies to achieve stress management:

6.2.1 RECOGNIZING STRESS TRIGGERS:

Assist your teenager in identifying the specific factors that trigger their stress. These triggers vary for each individual and may include changes in routine, sensory overload, social situations, academic pressures, or transitions. By understanding their stress triggers, they can begin implementing strategies to effectively manage them.

Encourage them to maintain a stress journal where they can document situations or events that elevate their stress levels. This awareness will help them develop targeted stress management techniques.

6.2.2 RELAXATION TECHNIQUES:

Teach your teenager various relaxation techniques to aid in stress management. Deep breathing exercises, progressive muscle relaxation, and guided imagery can effectively promote relaxation and reduce anxiety. Encourage regular practice of these techniques during stressful moments and as part of their daily routine.

Additionally, activities like yoga, meditation, or mindfulness exercises can foster relaxation and a sense of calm. Numerous resources, apps, and online videos are available specifically designed for individuals with autism to support their relaxation practice.

6.2.3 TIME MANAGEMENT AND ORGANIZATION:

Support your teenager in developing effective time management and organizational skills. Help them establish a structured routine that includes time for schoolwork, hobbies, relaxation, and social activities. Breaking tasks into manageable segments and utilizing visual schedules or calendars can help alleviate stress related to deadlines and responsibilities.

Teach them strategies for prioritizing tasks, setting goals, and managing their time effectively. Having a clear plan and an organized approach can reduce the feeling of being overwhelmed and increase their sense of control.

6.2.4 PHYSICAL ACTIVITY AND RECREATION:

Encourage regular physical activity as a means of managing stress. Engaging in activities such as walking, cycling, swimming, or playing sports can help release tension and improve mood. Physical exercise stimulates the production of endorphins, which are natural mood enhancers.

Support your teenager in finding recreational activities that they enjoy and align with their interests. Hobbies, creative outlets, and engaging in activities they are passionate about can serve as positive distractions from stressors and provide a sense of accomplishment.

6.2.5 SOCIAL SUPPORT AND CONNECTION:

Nurture social support and connections for your teenager. Encourage them to spend time with friends, join clubs or groups related to their interests, and participate in community activities. Social connections can provide a valuable support system and outlets for sharing experiences and emotions.

Ensure they have access to resources and support networks specifically designed for individuals with autism and their families. These communities can offer a sense of belonging and understanding, allowing them to share and learn from others who may be facing similar stressors.

6.2.6 HEALTHY LIFESTYLE HABITS:

Promote healthy lifestyle habits that contribute to stress management. Encourage your teenager to maintain a balanced diet, ensuring they receive proper nutrition. Sufficient sleep is also crucial for managing stress, so establish consistent bedtime routines that allow for adequate rest.

Limit exposure to excessive screen time and encourage activities that promote relaxation, such as reading, listening to calming music, or engaging in creative pursuits. Emphasize the importance of self-care, focusing on activities that bring them joy and relaxation.

6.2.7 SEEKING SUPPORT:

Encourage your teenager to seek support when needed. Let them know it is acceptable to ask for help from trusted adults, such as parents, teachers, or mental health professionals. Teach them to recognize when stress becomes overwhelming and when additional support may be necessary.

Collaborate with educators and professionals to create a supportive network that can assist your teenager in managing stress. This may involve

working with school counselors,
therapists, or participating in support
groups specifically tailored to teenagers
with autism.

Provide them with resources and
information about available mental
health services and professionals
specializing in supporting individuals
with autism. Encourage your teenager
to express their needs and concerns to
these professionals, as they can provide
guidance and strategies for stress
management.

Additionally, foster open communication and create a safe and non-judgmental environment where your teenager feels comfortable discussing their stressors and seeking support. Be an attentive listener and validate their feelings, offering empathy and understanding.

Remember that stress management techniques vary for each individual, and it may take time to find the strategies that work best for your teenager.

Encourage them to experiment with different techniques and adapt them to their unique needs and preferences.

By empowering your teenager with effective stress management techniques, you can help them navigate the challenges of daily life with greater resilience and well-being. With your support and guidance, they can develop valuable skills to manage stress, prioritize self-care, and maintain a positive outlook even in the face of difficulties.

CHAPTER 7

TRANSITIONING TO ADULTHOOD

7.1 POST-SECONDARY EDUCATION AND VOCATIONAL OPPORTUNITIES – PARAPHRASED:

The transition to adulthood is a significant milestone for teenagers with autism. It's important to help them navigate this phase by exploring educational and vocational possibilities that align with their interests, abilities, and goals. Here are some key considerations and strategies to support teenagers with autism during this transition:

7.1.1 EXPLORING OPTIONS FOR HIGHER EDUCATION:

Encourage your teenager to explore different paths for higher education, such as colleges, universities, vocational schools, or specialized programs. Assist them in researching and gathering information about the programs, admission requirements, support services, and resources available for individuals with autism.

Attend college fairs, open houses, and information sessions specifically

tailored to students with disabilities.
These events provide valuable
opportunities to connect with
representatives, ask questions, and gain
a better understanding of the available
educational opportunities.

7.1.2 CUSTOMIZED EDUCATION AND SUPPORT:

Collaborate with educators, counselors, and disability support services at post-secondary institutions to create an individualized education plan (IEP) or a 504 plan that outlines the accommodations and support your teenager may need. This plan will ensure their access to necessary resources, assistive technologies, and academic assistance throughout their college or vocational journey.

Empower your teenager to advocate for themselves and communicate their needs to professors, administrators, and disability support staff. Encourage them to request accommodations, modifications, or additional support whenever required.

7.1.3 TRANSITION PROGRAMS AND SUPPORT SERVICES:

Explore transition programs and support services specifically designed for students with autism. Many colleges and universities offer comprehensive support programs that include academic assistance, social skills training, counseling, and peer mentorship.

These programs can facilitate a smooth transition and provide a supportive environment where your teenager can thrive academically, socially, and emotionally. Research the availability of these programs and their track record in supporting students with autism.

7.1.4 VOCATIONAL OPPORTUNITIES AND JOB TRAINING:

Investigate vocational opportunities that align with your teenager's strengths, interests, and career aspirations. Vocational training programs, apprenticeships, or internships can provide valuable hands-on experience and develop specific skills in areas such as technology, trades, arts, or healthcare.

Collaborate with vocational
rehabilitation agencies, job coaches, and
transition specialists who can guide
your teenager in finding suitable
employment and help them develop job-
seeking skills, build a resume, and
improve interview techniques.

7.1.5 COLLEGE READINESS AND LIFE SKILLS:

Prepare your teenager for the transition to higher education by assisting them in developing essential college readiness and life skills. Focus on areas such as organization, time management, study skills, self-advocacy, and independent living skills.

Encourage their participation in programs or workshops that specifically address these skill sets. Practice real-life scenarios, such as managing finances, navigating transportation, and maintaining personal well-being, to foster independence and self-sufficiency.

7.1.6 SEEKING MENTORSHIP AND BUILDING NETWORKS:

Connect your teenager with mentors or individuals who have successfully navigated higher education or vocational paths. Mentorship can provide valuable guidance, inspiration, and practical advice.

Encourage your teenager to join autism support networks, online communities, or student organizations where they can connect with peers who share similar experiences and aspirations. These connections can offer support, networking opportunities, and a sense of belonging.

Remember, the transition to higher education or vocational opportunities may present challenges and require adjustments. It is crucial to maintain open communication, provide ongoing support, and adapt strategies as needed to ensure your teenager's success and well-being.

By exploring higher education and vocational opportunities and providing the necessary support, you can empower your teenager with autism to pursue their passions, achieve their goals, and thrive in their chosen career paths.

7.2 INDEPENDENT LIVING AND HOUSING OPTIONS:

When teenagers on the autism spectrum transition into adulthood, it's crucial to consider their ability to live independently and explore housing choices. This stage offers a chance for them to develop vital life skills, foster self-reliance, and discover various living arrangements that promote their autonomy and well-being. Here are key factors and strategies for supporting teenagers with autism as they embark on their journey toward independent living:

7.2.1 ASSESSING READINESS FOR INDEPENDENT LIVING:

Evaluate your teenager's preparedness for independent living by assessing their maturity level, self-care abilities, capacity to handle daily tasks, and overall independence. Identify their strengths and areas for improvement to determine the appropriate level of support and assistance they may require in their living situation.

Seek input from professionals specializing in supporting individuals with autism during the transition to independent living, such as therapists, counselors, or social workers. They can provide valuable insights and personalized guidance tailored to your teenager's unique needs.

7.2.2 TRANSITION PLANNING AND SKILL DEVELOPMENT:

Develop a transition plan that outlines specific goals and milestones for independent living. Collaborate with your teenager to identify areas they need to focus on, such as managing finances, meal planning and preparation, housekeeping, personal hygiene, transportation, and social skills.

Work together to cultivate these essential life skills through structured learning opportunities, practical experiences, and guided practice. Utilize visual aids, social stories, or task analysis to break down complex tasks into manageable steps, fostering independence and confidence.

7.2.3 EXPLORING HOUSING OPTIONS:

Research different housing options catering to individuals with autism that provide the necessary support for independent living. These options may include:

Supported living arrangements: These programs combine independent living with on-site support staff who offer guidance, assistance, and supervision based on individual needs.

Shared living or roommate arrangements: Encourage your teenager to consider sharing a living space with peers or individuals who share similar interests and support requirements. This arrangement can provide a sense of community and social connections.

Transitional living programs: These programs bridge the gap between dependence and complete independence.

Typically, they offer structured support, life skills training, and supervision to help teenagers gradually transition to independent living.

Community-based services: Explore community resources and programs that offer assistance with housing, independent living skills, and support services for individuals with autism.

Ensure that the chosen housing option aligns with your teenager's preferences, needs, and comfort level. Visit potential living spaces, engage in conversations with program coordinators or administrators, and inquire about the level of support, safety measures, and opportunities for community integration.

7.2.4 BUILDING SUPPORT NETWORKS:

Encourage your teenager to establish a support network in their chosen living environment. This network may include neighbors, roommates, support staff, or mentors who can offer guidance, companionship, and assistance when necessary.

Connect with local autism organizations, support groups, or social clubs that provide opportunities for socializing, networking, and community engagement. These connections can foster a sense of belonging and provide a support system outside of the immediate living environment.

7.2.5 FINANCIAL PLANNING AND BUDGETING:

Guide your teenager in understanding financial responsibilities and developing budgeting skills. Teach them the importance of managing finances, paying bills, and setting financial goals.

Introduce them to resources and tools that can aid in financial planning, such as budgeting apps, online resources, or financial literacy programs. Encourage them to seek professional advice if needed to ensure a secure financial future.

7.2.6 SAFETY AND EMERGENCY PREPAREDNESS:

Educate your teenager about safety measures and emergency preparedness in their living environment. Discuss topics such as home safety, personal security, fire safety, and appropriate responses during emergencies.

Collaborate on developing a safety plan that outlines emergency contacts, evacuation procedures, and strategies for handling unexpected situations. Regular reviews and practice drills can help your teenager become familiar with emergency protocols and feel more confident in their ability to manage potential risks.

7.2.7 ONGOING SUPPORT AND MONITORING:

While promoting independent living, it's crucial to maintain ongoing support and monitoring to ensure your teenager's well-being and success. Stay involved in their life, providing guidance and assistance as needed, while gradually allowing them to take on more responsibilities and make independent decisions.

Regular check-ins and open communication can help address any challenges or concerns that arise. Encourage your teenager to express their needs and advocate for themselves, while also being available to offer guidance, problem-solving strategies, and emotional support.

7.2.8 SEEKING PROFESSIONAL GUIDANCE:

If you are uncertain about the best independent living options or need further guidance, consult professionals specializing in supporting individuals with autism during the transition to independent living. They can provide expert advice, resources, and assistance in navigating the various housing options and support services available.

Additionally, consider connecting with support organizations or advocacy groups focused on independent living for individuals with autism. These organizations can offer valuable insights, share experiences, and provide resources specific to your teenager's needs.

By promoting independent living and exploring suitable housing options, you empower your teenager on the autism spectrum to develop essential life skills, gain self-confidence, and experience personal growth. With the right support and planning, they can thrive in a living environment that aligns with their abilities, goals, and aspirations.

7.3 LEGAL RIGHTS AND ADVOCACY:

As teenagers with autism spectrum disorder transition into adulthood, it is vital to comprehend their legal rights and actively support their needs and interests. By familiarizing yourself with the laws and regulations that safeguard individuals with autism, you can ensure that your teenager receives the necessary accommodations, support, and opportunities. Here are essential considerations and strategies for

navigating legal rights and advocacy:

7.3.1 EDUCATE YOURSELF:

Take the initiative to acquaint yourself with the laws and regulations that protect the rights of individuals with autism, such as the Americans with Disabilities Act (ADA), Section 504 of the Rehabilitation Act, and the Individuals with Disabilities Education Act (IDEA). Having a solid understanding of these laws will empower you to effectively advocate for your teenager's rights in different areas, including education, employment, housing, and public services.

Stay informed about any legislative updates or changes that may impact the rights and entitlements of individuals with autism. Utilize reliable online resources, participate in workshops or conferences, and connect with local autism organizations to stay up to date.

7.3.2 IEP TRANSITION PLANNING:

If your teenager has an Individualized Education Program (IEP), ensure that transition planning is incorporated as they approach adulthood. Collaborate with the IEP team, which includes educators, counselors, and transition specialists, to develop a transition plan that outlines goals, accommodations, and support services to facilitate a smooth transition into adulthood.

Advocate for appropriate services and support that will enable your teenager to achieve their post-secondary education or vocational goals. This may involve accommodations for standardized tests, transition-focused courses, career counseling, and connections to community resources.

7.3.3 EMPLOYMENT RIGHTS AND ACCOMMODATIONS:

Comprehend the legal protections that individuals with autism have in the workplace. The ADA prohibits employment discrimination based on disability and requires employers to provide reasonable accommodations to individuals with disabilities, including autism, to perform essential job functions.

Research employment laws specific to your region or country to ensure that your teenager's rights are protected in terms of hiring, workplace accommodations, and equal opportunities. Familiarize yourself with the process of requesting accommodations and collaborate with your teenager to develop their self-advocacy skills in the workplace.

7.3.4 GUARDIANSHIP AND DECISION-MAKING:

As your teenager approaches the age of majority, it is important to consider legal decision-making and guardianship. Depending on your teenager's level of independence and capacity to make informed decisions, you may need to explore options for guardianship or alternative decision-making models.

Consult with legal professionals specializing in disability law to understand the available options and determine the best approach to ensuring your teenager's well-being and autonomy.

7.3.5 ACCESSING SUPPORT SERVICES:

Be aware of the support services available for individuals with autism and their families. Research funding sources, government programs, and community resources that can provide financial assistance, respite care, vocational training, or housing support.

Advocate for your teenager's access to these support services, ensuring that they receive the necessary assistance to lead a fulfilling and independent life.

Stay informed about eligibility criteria,

application processes, and the available

supports in your area.

7.3.6 BUILDING A SUPPORTIVE NETWORK:

Connect with local and national autism advocacy organizations, support groups, and parent networks. These groups can offer valuable guidance, resources, and opportunities to collaborate with other families facing similar challenges.

Join forces with other advocates to raise awareness, influence policy changes, and advocate for improved services and support for individuals with autism. By working together, you can amplify your collective voice and drive positive change.

Remember, being an effective advocate for your teenager requires continuous education, collaboration, and perseverance. Stay informed, seek support when needed, and empower your teenager to advocate for themselves as they gain more independence.

By understanding legal rights, advocating for necessary accommodations, and actively participating in their transition to adulthood, you can help ensure that your teenager on the autism spectrum receives the support they need to thrive and lead a fulfilling life.

CHAPTER 8

RESOURCES AND SUPPORT

8.1 ORGANIZATIONS AND WEBSITES:

When it comes to providing assistance to teenagers with autism, there is a wide range of resources accessible through different organizations and websites.

These platforms offer valuable information, support systems, and tools to aid individuals with autism, their families, educators, and professionals involved in their lives. Here are some noteworthy organizations and websites that focus on supporting and advocating for autism:

Autism Speaks: With its website at www.autismspeaks.org, Autism Speaks is one of the largest autism advocacy organizations. It provides an extensive array of resources, support services, and research initiatives. Their website offers comprehensive information on autism, strategies for early intervention, treatment options, and a directory of local resources.

Autism Society: The Autism Society, found at www.autism-society.org, is a grassroots organization that promotes advocacy, support, and inclusion for individuals with autism and their families. Their website provides resources on education, transition planning, employment, and community engagement.

- National Autism Association: Focusing on providing support, education, and advocacy, the National Autism Association, accessible at www.nationalautismassociation.org, serves individuals with autism and their families. Their website offers resources on safety, prevention of wandering, and community outreach.

- Autism NOW Center: The Autism NOW Center is a national resource and information center that addresses various aspects of autism, such as education, employment, housing, and community living. Their website at www.autismnow.org provides comprehensive resources, webinars, and tools for individuals with autism, self-advocates, and family members.

- The Arc: The Arc is an organization that advocates for the rights and inclusion of individuals with intellectual and developmental disabilities, including autism. Their website, www.thearc.org, offers information on legal rights, advocacy, and local chapters that provide support services and resources.

- The Autism Self Advocacy Network (ASAN): ASAN is a self-advocacy organization operated by individuals on the autism spectrum. Their website at www.autisticadvocacy.org features resources, toolkits, and personal stories that promote self-

advocacy, inclusion, and
empowerment.

- Autism Society of America: The
Autism Society of America provides
support and resources for individuals
with autism and their families. Their
website, www.autism-society.org,
offers information on advocacy, local
chapters, and community events.

- Interactive Autism Network (IAN):
IAN is an online research network
that connects individuals with autism

and their families with researchers.
Their website at
www.iancommunity.org features
resources, research studies, and a
community forum for sharing
experiences and support.

- Autism Research Institute (ARI):
ARI focuses on research, treatment,
and education for individuals with
autism. Their website,
www.autism.org, provides
information on biomedical

interventions, conferences, and webinars.

● My Autism Team: My Autism Team is a social network for individuals with autism and their families, accessible at www.myautismteam.com. It allows users to connect, share experiences, and find support from others who understand their journey.

These organizations and websites offer various resources, support networks, and updated information on autism-related subjects. Take advantage of their offerings to enhance your knowledge, connect with others, and access valuable tools and services.

Remember to always assess the credibility and relevance of the information you find, as the field of autism research and support is continually evolving. Additionally, reach out to local autism organizations and professionals in your community for additional resources tailored to your teenager's specific needs and interests.

By utilizing these resources and support networks, you can gain valuable insights, access relevant information, and connect with a community that understands and supports individuals on the autism spectrum.

8.2 SUPPORT GROUPS AND COMMUNITY SERVICES

Support groups and community services play a vital role in supporting individuals with autism and their families by providing practical assistance, emotional support, and a sense of belonging. These groups offer a platform for sharing experiences, seeking guidance, and connecting with others who understand the unique challenges and successes associated with autism. Here are some key aspects

of support groups and community
services:

- Local Autism Support Groups: Many
communities have support groups
specifically designed for individuals
with autism and their families. These
groups regularly organize meetings,
workshops, and social activities
where members can share
experiences, exchange advice, and
support each other. Joining a local
support group can provide a valuable
network of understanding individuals

who can offer guidance, resources, and emotional support.

- Online Support Communities: In addition to local support groups, online communities and forums provide a convenient way to connect with individuals worldwide who are facing similar experiences. Platforms like Facebook groups, online forums, and dedicated autism support websites offer spaces for asking questions, sharing stories, and finding support from a diverse community. Online communities are particularly helpful for those with limited access to local resources or a preference for online interactions.

- Parent and Caregiver Support Groups: These groups focus on addressing the unique challenges and concerns faced by parents and caregivers of individuals with autism. They provide a safe and supportive environment to discuss experiences, seek advice, and learn from one another. Sharing stories and

strategies can help alleviate feelings
of isolation and provide practical tips
for navigating various aspects of
raising a child with autism.

- Sibling Support Programs: Siblings
  of individuals with autism also
  benefit from support networks that
  acknowledge their unique
  experiences and challenges. Sibling
  support programs create spaces for
  siblings to connect, share their
  feelings, and gain support from
  others who understand their

perspective. These programs may
offer workshops, recreational
activities, and counseling services to
help siblings navigate their roles and
build strong relationships.

- Community Services and Programs:
Many communities offer specialized
services and programs tailored to
support individuals with autism and
their families. These can include
recreational programs, therapeutic
services, respite care, vocational
training, and opportunities for social

skills development. Local community centers, autism organizations, and government agencies often provide information and resources to help individuals access these services.

- Advocacy and Awareness Groups: Advocacy and awareness groups play a vital role in promoting understanding, acceptance, and inclusion for individuals with autism. These groups work to raise public awareness, influence policy changes, and advocate for the rights and needs of individuals on the autism spectrum. Connecting with advocacy groups can provide opportunities to participate in campaigns, educational events, and legislative efforts aimed at creating a more inclusive society.

When looking for support groups and community services, consider factors such as location, specific areas of interest or need, and the preferences of your teenager and family. Reach out to local autism organizations, schools, and healthcare professionals to inquire about available services and recommended support groups in your area.

Remember that each support group or community service may have its own unique focus and approach. It's important to find a group or service that aligns with your teenager's specific needs and interests. Participating in these groups and accessing community services can provide a sense of belonging, emotional support, and practical resources to help your teenager and family navigate the autism journey with greater confidence and resilience.

CONCLUSION

EMBRACING NEURODIVERSITY AND CELEBRATING INDIVIDUALITY

In this guide, we have delved into various aspects of supporting and empowering teenagers with autism. An underlying message throughout has been the significance of embracing neurodiversity and honoring the unique strengths, talents, and perspectives of individuals with autism. By acknowledging and appreciating the diversity of human cognition, we can cultivate a society that values and includes individuals on the autism spectrum.

It is essential to shift our mindset away from perceiving autism as a disorder requiring fixing or curing, and instead recognize it as a natural variation in human neurology. Embracing neurodiversity means recognizing that each person possesses their own strengths, challenges, and ways of perceiving the world. By fostering inclusivity and creating environments that accommodate diverse needs and communication styles, we can empower teenagers with autism to realize their full potential.

Inclusive education, community programs, and workplaces that embrace neurodiversity offer opportunities for individuals with autism to flourish and contribute their unique talents. By appreciating the strengths and abilities of those on the autism spectrum, we can establish a society that benefits from the richness of human minds and experiences.

HOPE FOR THE FUTURE

As a matter of fact, it is important to acknowledge that there is hope for a brighter future for individuals on the autism spectrum. Advancements in research, education, and advocacy have led to increased awareness, understanding, and support for individuals with autism. The growing acceptance of neurodiversity and efforts to create inclusive communities provide us with optimism for a more inclusive and equitable future.

Teenagers with autism have immense potential, and with the right support, they can overcome challenges, pursue their passions, and lead fulfilling lives. It is crucial to provide them with the tools, resources, and opportunities they need to develop their independence, self-advocacy skills, and social connections.

By nurturing positive relationships, fostering supportive environments, and collaborating with educators, professionals, and the community, we can establish a comprehensive support system that empowers teenagers with autism to thrive. Together, we can dismantle barriers, challenge stereotypes, and build a world where individuals on the autism spectrum are valued, respected, and included.

As we embark on the journey of empowering teenagers with autism, let us continue to learn, grow, and advocate for their rights and well-being. By embracing neurodiversity, celebrating individuality, and fostering a culture of acceptance, we can create a more inclusive and promising future for all.